I0424465

A True Story About
The Parolee

By Darren Johnson

authorHOUSE®

AuthorHouse™
1663 Liberty Drive, Suite 200
Bloomington, IN 47403
www.authorhouse.com
Phone: 1-800-839-8640

© 2009 Darren Johnson. All rights reserved.

No part of this book may be reproduced, stored in
a retrieval system, or transmitted by any means
without the written permission of the author.

First published by AuthorHouse 11/9/2009

ISBN: 978-1-4490-4310-0 (e)
ISBN: 978-1-4490-4328-5 (sc)

Printed in the United States of America
Bloomington, Indiana

This book is printed on acid-free paper.

Letter from the Author

I would like to say thank you for taking this time to read my book. I have poured a lot into writing this book. I have shared so much of myself with you in these pages. But I must stop and say thank you to God for giving me the ability to write, I must say thank you to my wonderful & loving wife. You are the very essence of my being. I love every inch of you. I wish to make your every dream come true! Thank you baby for suggesting I write this book!

Darren Johnson
Your Husband
I Love You

THE PAROLEE

It's now March 11, 2004. It's been 8 long years. Six crazy prisons with countless riots. Two county jails and a whole lot of crooked cops. But this is all over now. Because I have just paroled from prison.

My name is Darren let me tell you my story. You see I got locked up August 26, 1996 for a crime that I didn't commit. I was rail-roaded by the Pomona superior court system. The judge knew I was not guilty but because I am black, I was going to prison. My own state appointed attorney who did not represent me. He made sure that I went to prison. I was very angry but what could I do? So I went back to the Los Angels county jail to a wait the bus for prison. As the bus rolled out of Pomona on the freeway, I just looked out the window in awe! I could not believe what was going on. I was going to jail for rape then I would have to walk the prison yard and pray I didn't get stuck with something. So I developed a nasty, nasty, nasty attitude. I had to keep everyone far away from me if I wanted so survive. My attitude began to get worse and worse with every passing day. So by the time I left the county jail headed for prison I was not to be played with. I knew the best way to do this time in peace was to put the smash down when I had to. So others would fear. Well the bus came to take me to prison. I arrived at Delano State prison, got classified. I was sent to Soledad to do my time. I was all shook up over the whole thing. But I could not show this to anyone. I rode the bus early in the morning to Soledad. The bus ride was long and cold and very quiet. The police would not allow any talking on the bus. They threaten to pull over and beat us up while we were handcuffed hand and foot. When we got to Soledad they locked us up in cells for a month. When I finally was allowed to come out and go to the yard, I saw a white man get stabbed over 40 times. They killed him. They said, "he was a child molester". But came to find he was not. They had moved the child molester in the middle of the night and put this other guy in his cell. I was truly stunned at all this! I could not say a word about why I was locked up! Especially after seeing this, well things were going really well. I would chill with the Fellas from the Los Angeles gangs! All of the gangsters hung together. I did not have any problems. Everything was fine till August 1997 that's when the courts brought me back. Pomona sent for me to come to court. They had arrested the person they say I had helped. So I went back so court. But it was really strange. They found out that the crime did not happen! The Jury came back with a not guilty verdict.

So the case was dismissed. But they refused to release me from prison. They sent me back to prison for a crime that they found out never happened. I was angry. How could California do this to me I thought. Then I looked in the mirror and said "I know how and why, because I'm black. They know I did not commit this crime but I still go to prison. Well they put me on a bus and sent me back to Soledad. I stayed there for another year then transferred to C.M.C. where I paroled from March of 1999. I got out super angry but held it deeply inside. When I got out my baby brother and his girl friend came to pick me up from the bus station.

It felt real strange now to be out. So I did push ups as I waited for them to show up. Not long after I started my push-ups they pulled up! I was very happy to see my brother. He was happy to see me as well. He asked me how many push-ups did I just do? I said, "only a thousand." I did 10 sets of 50 twice. He said, "you look cool". I thanked him and we got in the car and left. He then introduced me to his girlfriend. We then drove to my parents' house for a quick second so I could see them.

We stayed there for a short time then went over to his house in Redlands. When we all got out at his house I noticed his girlfriend was pregnant. I asked when was the baby due? They said July. Then my brother asked me had I spoken to my other brother in Texas? I said "no, not yet". He then asked had I spoken to my daughter. I said "no". He then asked was there anything I wanted to do. I said no not really because I need to go and see my parole officer in the morning.

He said alright I'll take you. We then went to sleep. The next day we went to see my parole officer. He seemed alright when I first met him! So I thought but I would soon find out the truth. Especially, since I was hanging out with my brother. He had no job and always smoking weed. He had cut off notices on the house. I was like what's up with this? He didn't have any solution for his problems. I had to do something quick. So I put together a plan to rob a store. He was with it until I did the robbery then he didn't want to do it. But it was too late now! He drove the car for me and we got stopped. I was headed right to prison. But this time I did it. I went to court and the judge gave me 5 years. I was in the county jail waiting to go to prison when my parole officer came to see me with a report he wrote.

It said I got out looking for trouble. He had lied, because I had got out trying to help my brother. But according to him that was not the case! So here I go again back to prison. I spent the next 5 years in prison getting angrier and angrier. Well finally the day came that I have been waiting for March 11, 2004. I had another date but I lost it by getting into trouble! But I managed to hold on to this one. I was finally out. But really didn't even realize what I was in for! the parolee. That is a whole new world I mean truly to be on parole is really, truly rough. I would soon find out just how rough. Now I thought about the last time I was at this same point in my life. If did not work because 27 days later I was back in prison. I was determined not to allow that too happened again to me. So as I waited for the police to give me my own clothes. So I could take off these prison clothes for the very last time. My mind raced as to what I wanted to do first.

The police came with my clothes and I got dressed. Then he came back with 200 hundred dollars and said you'll be back. I said, "You're crazy." We then got in the van and headed for the releasing area. There was some guy from the Walden House there to pick me up because I had chosen to go to this program for parolees because I had been in prison for so long. He introduced himself as we waited for my final papers from this prison. But there was a problem with my paperwork. They were not going to allow me to leave. I got real mad. The guy from Walden House said it will be alright, the police said "okay you can go." We walked out the bars and the gates. I was a free man so I thought I really had no idea what it meant to be on parole. Let alone to be on parole in Los Angeles, California. But I would soon find out just what that truly meant and believe me it was a very bad thing that I found out. I and the guy Walden House sent to pick me up drove away from the prison. He asked did I want to stop anywhere. I said no and we headed straight for the freeway. I was glad I just wanted to get away from the prison. I didn't want to stay in this area one minute more than it was necessary. So we hit the freeway. We arrived at the Walden House Downtown Los Angeles sometime that day. I saw a lot of the guys from prison. It felt like I was back in prison seeing all these same dudes here. A lot of us had signed up for Walden House in prison and had stated we would go when we paroled. But to see all these same dudes. Man I was so cool. I was ready to leave as soon as I saw these dudes. But a few of the counselors talked to me and said just give it a try. I had met a few of them while I was still in prison. They seemed real cool while I was talking to them. So I said alright I'll give it a chance. I then went and put my things in the room they had for me. I came down stairs and began filling out some papers they had for me. They told me I had to go see my parole officer. I and another parolee grabbed a bus pass and headed for the parole office. As we rode the bus he began to tell me about Walden House. He said it was just like the pen. But it gets better offer about 3 months. I told him I was not going to be going through no prison drama on the streets.

He said yeah I feel you man. This parole thing is hard out here if you have the wrong P.O. I said the wrong parole officer what do you mean by that? He said some of parole officers are a trip. They have super bad attitudes watch you'll see. I said I hope I get a good one.

He asked who do you have? I replied Mendoza. He said Ah man he's a cold piece of work. That Dude will cross you up and have you back in the pen, be careful with him. I was like he can't be that bad. He said, "You'll see! Listen this is our stop. I said this is it right here. He said yeah as we exited the bus. We walked in the building and he showed me where to sign in. After about an hour Mendoza called me in. He gave me some speech about his rules and expectations. Then took pitchers of me! He then asked had I registered.

I said I have an appointment in a couple of days. He replied when you register bring me the papers or I'll send you straight back to prison am I clear? I said "yeah I hear you. He said alright you can go now. I opened the door of his office and walked out. The guy who came with me said how was it? I said that man is straight crazy. He said I told you Mendoza was a fool. I said I didn't think it was as bad as you said, but that dude is straight crazy. We finished talking and walked back to the bus stop. We caught the bus back to Walden House. When I went inside this time it was full of dudes I knew from prison. I was like this might not be so bad. But it was too much like prison, there was no freedom at all. But I told myself I could make it anywhere. I already had my plans as to what I was going to do. I was not going to allow no one to stop my plans. Especially not some parole officer or some dudes I knew from prison. Well things seemed to be alright. I went to the police station the next day took care of my registration.

When I returned back to Walden House my parole officer was there. He wanted to see my registration card. I was like man I just got back from the police department and you are already here man. He said yeah I'll be popping up whenever I feel like it Mr. Johnson so may be I can send you back to prison. I said you don't have any reason to try and violate me. He said just don't let me catch you doing anything. I said, "yeah whatever", then he left.

Some of the other guys said man you got him I feel for you. I said, "Why is that? They said because he loves to violate people watch you'll see. I said I am going to see nothing I'm going to stay away from him. They said that will be your best bet. I began to put my plan together. Everything was going alright so far till I began to have problems with different people telling me I could not do certain things. So I knew it was time to go. I had gotten the female I wanted. Now I just had to put things right. She was behind me and my sole supporter. No one else gave me any support but her. I fell in love with her. We would talk everyday but we had to talk for 15 minutes at a time because that's the way Walden House's phones were set up, just like prison. So I was cool with that. I was really tired of prison and I wanted nothing that reminded me of prison. But I felt I could handle these little things, but the little things were starting to get to me.

Especially since I was having such problems with this parole officers and this place acting like it was prison. Till I almost had to whoop on the biggest dude in Walden House over the phone!

I think he thought I was scared! Because everyone else was. I stood up and told him

"Nigga you'll touch everything in this room trying to get away from me". The counselors ran down but they were afraid to get in between us. I knew he really didn't want to get down when he turned and walked away with the counselor. I could still hear him talking but it was real low. I just went upstairs to my room and thought to myself why was I putting up with program place? Then I decided to go to bed. The next day the main counselors called us in the office. We talked about the situation and found out it was a big misunderstanding. We shook hands and it was over! We both walked out together. Everyone was asking what happen? We just said a misunderstanding that's all and kept walking. We went outside in the back and talked.

He was like man what's up with you. We have been cool all this time. So what's the problem? I said this parole thing is killing me, that parole agent is really trying to cross me up. I just did 8½ years straight. Man I'm cool you feel me? He said, "I knew it was something bothering you. I could see it in your eyes last night.

I said yeah! Say man I'm cool with this place I'm out of here. He said, "no man it's not that bad". I said, "I'm gone", and then I walked away. I went upstairs to my room as I went to my room a few people would ask if I was alright. I just looked through them. I guess my eyes told them to stay far away. I was not playing. I walked straight out the door. I told then I was cool. They tried to stop me at the door. I told them if they put their hands on me they would not touch no one else.

They moved out of my way. I walked down to the bus stop. I found a pay phone to call my parole officer. He was like you better get back to Walden House before I send the police to pick you up. Where are you? That's when I hung up the phone on him and jumped on the bus. I was headed to see any girl. She did not even know I was on my way! I got out there with her that night. She was shocked to see me. We talked and she said you have to do what they want because they'll violate you. After listening to her I realized she was right. So I called my parole officer and spoke to him! I told him I would come back. He said he would recall the warrant. I said warrant. He said' yeah I put a warrant out for your rest. If you return by Monday I'll recall it. I said alright I'll be there then hung up. I called Walden House and spoke to the weekend counselor. He said you can come back but you have to take a drug test and take a 30 day punishment.

I said alright I am tripping on that and I'll see you on Monday. Then I hung up the phone. I told my girl what was going on. She said it will be alright. I said yeah, I really don't need problems with that parole officer.

She said yeah that guy is mean. We then got ready to drive back to Los Angeles. I had caught the bus to my girl's house in Rialto. Well Monday came and we drove to Los Angeles back to Walden House. I kissed my girl and walked inside the building. Everyone was surprised to see me. They made their funny little comments about me using dope and being homeless. I just looked at them really serious. The week-end counselor told them please leave him alone we do not need any problems.

I told him I was not even tripping on these dudes. I just don't want problems with my parole officer. He said oh, by the way he was here earlier today. I was like man this dude is all over me. The weekend counselor said yeah I see, well come on you have to take the drug test. We went to the restroom and took the drug test. It came back in a couple of minutes. It was clean. I told the counselor I don't use drugs. He said why did you leave? I said because I left prison in March I don't want to keep feeling it. He said just trust the process the program works. I said I came back because my parole officer is trying to violate me. That's the only reason. I am not going to allow it to happen. He said well you should still trust the process. I said alright let's see this process. I went through their 30 day punishment. I got off the punishment and started trying to put my life back together. I had some rough roads to travel. I was doing really well. Things were coming together for me, but the parole officer kept shutting down every door for me. Every chance for me to do something the parole officer would say no!

I was really getting tired of this parole officer. He was over doing his job. Man it didn't take all that what he was doing. Then they started really tripping at Walden House because the counselors knew my parole officer wanted to send me back to prison. They wanted to push any button to make me trip. They did and I packed all my stuff and left for good. They said we're calling your parole officer and let him know you left again. I said do you think I care. I am not mandated to be in no program. So you can call who you want. I then walked outside with my things. I called me a fox and went right back to Rialto with my girl. When I got her apartment she was shocked. She said' what are you doing here? I explained to her I was cool with all these fake dudes out here plus that crazy parole officer. Man I am so cool with all of this. It's the very same thing in prison. Everyone has a story and they all try to trap you up. So I'm cool baby!

She said yeah, but you can't just let that parole officer put you back in prison. I said yeah, I know, but I will not go back to some program that I do not have to be in anyway just for him. She said you know something let's pray and ask God to help us. I said alright that's a good idea. We then held hands and began to pray that God would help us. After we finished praying my girl said you should go and talk to your parole officer and explain you are not mandated to be in no program. Maybe he'll understand.

I said maybe he will, I'll call him. I then grabbed the phone and dialed his number, the phone rang and he answered to my surprise. I said this is Johnson K-36142. He replied Mr. Johnson where are you? You know you are on your way back to prison. I said' hold up I am not required to be in any program that was my choice. There's nothing that says I have to either. He replied oh, yes there is. I say you have to be. Remember you are a parolee I control what you do and don't do.

I said yeah, whatever so you are telling me that you are forcing me to do something the courts couldn't make me do! That's right he replied. I asked and how is that? He said because you are nothing but a parolee and I'm your parole officer so you do what I say. At that point I got very angry and hung up the phone on him.

My girl said call him back stupid he can lock you up don't do that. I thought about what she said and called him back. When he answered I said oh, we got disconnected. He said so what are you going to do Mr. Johnson? I said I'm on my way back. I'll be there. He said be at my office before 10'o clock p.m. I said yeah, I'll be there. So me and my girl got up and headed for Los Angles. We got there about 12 noon. I went into the parole officer's office. He was on the phone. He looked up and saw me and said, "Are you ready to go back to Walden House? I looked at him and said I told you on the phone that I was not required to be in no program. So I am not going. He said, you're not, so you're going back to prison. I said so you're going to violate me. He said' I am not violating you. You are violating you. By not doing what I said. I said hold up I need to go and talk to my girl.

He said alright you have 5 minutes. I then walked out of his office and began to explain what was going on to my girl. She said why is he pushing this program on you when you're not mandated to even be in one? I said I don't know. She said well what ever you have to do just do it.

I said he wants me to do it his way. But I'm cool with Walden House. She said do they have any other programs that would be better? I said I don't know. She said well you should go back in there and find out. I said alright. Then I walked back in his office. He said well Mr. Johnson what is your decision? I said is there any other program since you are so bent on sending me to this program? He said I have one and gave me the address. I took the address from him and me and my girl left to go find this program place. We talked as we drove. My girl said. Man your parole officer is making you go to this program. You should go to his supervisor Darren don't just let him do this to you. You have rights. I said yeah, but with his supervisor do? She said I don't know but you should talk to him and see. I said yeah, I'll see after we find this place. Just then we found the place. It looked really bad. It was in a drug infested area. Me and my girl both said, "Hell no". I told her there's no way I'm staying here. She said now will you speak to his supervisor? I said yeah, boo! As soon as we get back to his office!

We then drove away headed back to the parole office. We got back to his office and I walked in. He said Mr. Johnson did you check in? I said no, where is your supervisor because you are not to violate me because I'm not going to any program. He looked at me crazy and we walked down the hall to his supervisor's office. The supervisor was able to listen to the situation that was going on. He asked his parole agent what was the problem with this parolee? I mean this supervisor really wanted to know what was going on. So the parole officer began to tell his side of the story. I just listened to his talk then the supervisor asked me what was the problem? I started by saying the parole officer was a liar in what he just told you. The supervisor said oh really. I said yes! Because I am not mandated by the courts to be in any program but he's trying to force me to live in one. He said where do you live now? I said right now I live with my girl in Rialto. He asked where did my controlling case take place? I said in Redlands. He said that's San Bernardino, County.

I said yes sir it is! He looked at the parole agent and said give him a 30 day travel pass while you put his paperwork together for transfer. The parole agent said what sir! The supervisor said you heard me do what I said to do. The parole officer said come on Johnson. The supervisor said hold up you will treat this man with respect do you hear me? The parole officer said yes sir. Then he said to me Mr. Johnson come with me please. I thanked the supervisor and he gave me his card. He told me to feel free to use it if I had any other problems. I thanked him and walked down to my parole officer's office. I said that man was cool huh. The parole officer was like he's. Then he just stopped in mid sentence and asked me for the address in Rialto. I smiled and gave him the address. He filled out my travel pass paper and gave it to me. He then said you have to come to get a new pass every 30 days till your case is transferred to the Fontana Unit. I said alright no problem but what about that warrant you put out on me? He replied on that I'll have if recalled. He then handed me my pass. I took it and we both walked out of his office. I went to the lobby where my girl was waiting for me! She saw me smiling and asked what happen with the supervisor? I explained the supervisor said I didn't have to go to any program. In fact I didn't even have to live in Los Angeles. I and my girl just laughed because we knew my parole officer was mad, but couldn't do any thing to me! Things were beginning to look like better. The parolee had won in this case. For the very first time in history someone was there for the parolee.

So I and my girl headed back home. But we decided to stop and get some soul food because they do not have it in Rialto. Well it was time now to go put this plan into action. I knew with my skills I could get a good job. But I needed just a chance. Well that chance came the very next day. I called a place went filled out the application and got hired. I started working in a warehouse through an agency.

I let the boss know I could operate a forklift as well as I could drive the diesel trucks! He asked me was I serious or just kidding? I looked at him and said I don't have any time to be playing. He said' well I'll give you a chance to show me. I said when? He said right now. I said let's go. We walked outside to the yard dog. I laughed the boss said what's funny? I said because you think I'm kidding about doing what I do but you'll see! He watched as I climbed in and started the tractor! Then I asked which one do you want moved and where? He showed me the computer. I programmed it for the dock moves. The moves came up I began to shuffle trailers. He was shocked at how fast I could move the trailers. He stopped me and said how long have you been driving? I just laughed. He said listen we need you out here I'll pay you more to drive. I said alright.

I stayed in the yard the rest of the day. Then they said you have to work the dock two days and drive two days. I was not happy with that because, I wanted a driving position full time. But they didn't have one right now. So I was cool with that for a little while at least I had a job being that I was on parole. That was enough all by itself. The fact that I was a parolee I mean just being a parolee is not good, that is really a terrible thing to be stripped of all your rights. That was the thing they did not ever tell me about. They always said don't go to prison because it's a bad place. But what they don't tell you is that parole is worse than prison. I know I have been on parole for 34½ months right now. I have been through the ringer with this system. Every single day I learn something new about California and the justice system.

You know what I learn? I learned California is not the place to be on parole. You are treated like a second class citizen with no rights at all especially when you go to see your parole officer. They treat you real bad from the receptionist, to the agent, to the officer of the day. They all treat you bad. Hell, even if you call they talk bad to you. They will hang up in your face and not answer when you call back plus when the local police see you they ask are you on probation or parole? Now as soon as you say yes. You have just become public enemy No. 1. Now in case you have not guessed being on parole is very bad. Statistics say that 1 of every 3 males in California are on probation or parole!

I am giving you this information first hand. I have been to prison twice. I was locked in prison in 1997 and was released in 2004! I have been to several. But the hardest thing is beating this parole. But let me tell you something when you are on parole the state controls you. You have no say to in what you do. Let me give you an example. I told you earlier about my situation when I had to go to the supervisor.

Well that unit was Silver Lake and it closed. I was passed around like a piece of chicken at a weight watchers party. I mean really I had about 10 different parole agents. Seriously I was having a new agent every month. Every month I had to deal with a different attitude. They would just show up at my house whenever they wanted, they would call my house and harass my wife all the time. Like she was supposed to know where I am all the time. She got angry and told them look I'm not on parole. I have rights. They would back off her and say tell him to call immediately. She would give me the message and I would call them back. I would let them know not to call my house and upset my wife and kids! They did not like my attitude but I let them know I didn't like the way they called my house either! Then they would pull that power trip act and say Mr. Johnson you are on parole you do what we say. I said' are you crazy. But just then my girl would calm me down she had a way of doing that like no one else. I would listen to my girl. She always made sense. She would say don't let them lock you up. Watch how you talk to these parole agents they can lock you up. So I would change my whole attitude.

It was so good that I had the women I had. So I continued to play the game. Well this game had turned even worse because this new parole officer I had just got wanted to violate me because any first parole officer never re-called that warrant.

Yeah, I trusted he would recall the warrant and now I was about to go back to prison and I had not done a thing. I had to go to a board hearing and explain my case! The board heard the experience and said I could continue on parole! The parolee agent realized I was not a problem parolee. I was just trying to complete this parole. I had asked to be discharged at 13 months but my parole agent said no, you have to bring another 9 months before I even consider it.

I was like why do I have to bring 2 years? He said don't ask me, I'm the agent you're the parolee. I said yeah, I know. Say do I have to keep coming to Los Angeles to get these travel passes? He said no I don't mind driving out there I have another parolee who lives in the same area. This is your last visit to the office. I thought cool I don't have to drive to Los Angeles any more that's great. I let my girl know that we didn't have to make the drive to

Los Angeles anymore. She asked how come? I said he said he has other parolees out where we live so I don't have to come up here any more. She said that's wonderful for you. I said yeah, as we got in the car and headed back to Rialto. Everything was fine back at the house for a while. Well until one day I got a knock at the door. It was a Fontana parole officer with a bad attitude. I could tell as soon as I opened the door. He came in our apartment straight tripping talking about he was checking me out because my paperwork was in for a transfer. He said look I don't care if you smoke weed. Just let me know if you have any contact with the police.

I said I don't do drugs, is there anything else you need with me? He said no. I have to submit my papers to Los Angeles on you. I said well I'm going in my house now I've committed no crime. He said I don't like your attitude Mr. Johnson. I said I don't like you either so I'm going in with my daughters. He said I'll put you on my case load! Then he left me and my girl talked about his attitude. We both stated I hope he's not your new agent. A couple of days later my agent called from Los Angeles telling me I was denied to be transferred to Fontana. He didn't tell me why but he did ask did I get into it with the Fontana agent? I told him that some black dude came from Fontana with an attitude that I wasn't feeling.

The parole agent was like your on parole. You have got to understand you are a parolee. You don't have any rights. You cannot upset anyone you will be back in prison with this attitude. I said yeah, is that all you called to tell me? No he said. In fact I'll be there to see you tomorrow be home! I said I'll be here what time are you coming? He said I'll be by before noon. You just better be there when I show up. I said so you want to me to just sit in the house and wait for you.

He said now you get it you're a parolee you do what I say. I said is there anything else. He replied no. We hung up the phone my girl said why do you have a messed up attitude now? I said because on this parole they treat you like of child. They constantly remind you that you are a parolee and you have no rights. Then they constantly threaten you with going back to prison. They don't just leave you alone and let you live. They try everything they can to push buttons so they can lock you up. I mean I'm not bothering any one but I'm being constantly harassed all the time. She said well don't have that attitude with me I'm not trying to hurt you and neither are my children. You don't have to come at us foul. I said I am so sorry I do not mean to have a negative attitude with you and the girls. It's just the parole is killing me. She said well just do what they ask you'll be off soon. I said yeah, you're right. The next day I got up the girls had went to school already. I went in the kitchen and fried me and my girl some fish. We were eating the fish when a knock at the door come. I said who is it? The voice said parole agent. My girl said listen be nice he can lock you up. I answered okay boo, then opened the door. He said good morning my girl said good morning back. I said good morning. He said Mr. Johnson you are very hostile and have a very bad attitude. I said because you guys are always trying to cross me up. He said Mr. Johnson I have no reason to cross you up. In fact I want to see you get off parole and enjoy your life and your family. Honestly I do. You don't know how refreshing it is to have a good parolee on your case load! I never worry about getting calls from the police on you! I said are you supposed to. I told you, I am tired of jail and police. I am not going back. It seems every other agent I hold was trying his best to send me back. He said well I'll work with you to see about getting you off parole. I said alright it's been 15 months. He said I'll see what I can do but right now you have to see in the bottle. I grabbed the bottle and went to my bathroom. I finished and brought the bottle back to him! He said' alright I'll see you next month. I'll call you and let you know what day. I said alright as I opened the door to let him out. This was the routine for the next 12 months. Well it was supposed to be until I discharged which I thought would be soon since he said he was going to see about discharging me. But he called and said the state wanted 36 months from me on parole. So I was stuck there was nothing I could do. So I was cool anyway I had a parole agent who wasn't tripping with me. But everything went away wrong when my parole agent got sick! They went back to bouncing me around I don't know what kind of sickness he had, but he was out for some months! I had so many different agents it wasn't even funny. Then they finally found out my agent wasn't coming back they gave me this black female. She was the worse parole agent I had ever come in contact with. She called me and had a nasty attitude. It was like she hated her job and everybody. I said man how did I get you? She said Mr. Johnson they just gave me your file and it's all tore up! How are you on parole and suppose to be in L.A. Country but you live in Rialto? I said that's where I live. I don't live in Los Angeles County. She said well since I just look over case you will be moving back to Los Angeles County. I don't supervise in San Bernardino County. I said I'm not moving to Los Angeles County are you crazy. My family and everyone I deal with are in the Inland Empire. She said Mr. Johnson I need you to come to the office. I said I already had my monthly visit for this month. My girl said stop tripping stupid. I said look I'll be out there tomorrow then got off the phone. My girl said you're so stupid you won't learn till they lock you up and I'm not coming to visit you either because you're so stupid. I said you're right I'm almost off this anyway. She said yeah, so don't mess it up now. The next day we drove to L.A. I had to wait for about an hour for her to see me! She finally did. She was still with that stupid stuff talking about I had to move. I hurried up and called for her supervisor. Man did she get hot when I wanted him. But she had to get the supervisor. He came in and asked what the problem was.

She began to say his parole is L.A. County but he lives in Rialto I'm not going to Rialto. The supervisor said hold on relax. I said look sir I've been on parole since March 11, 2004 and its May 11, 2006. I've been in Rialto since June 2004 do you think I'm going to just pack up and leave my family for her because she says I have to live in L.A. County. I don't thinks so! The supervisor said alright work with me here. I'll give you travel passes to be in Rialto for 30 days at a time but you have to come pick them up here. I said no problem. He told the female parole agent to write my pass. I wish you could have seen her face. She was passed but couldn't do anything. I had won again the supervisor left the room. The female parole agent smirked and said I still don't supervise in San Bernardino. I said, I still don't live in Los Angeles, this woman was angry. She handed me my pass and I left this would be the scene every time I would come to pick up my travel pass! She would keep me waiting in the lobby for a long time then call me in with my travel pass in her hand but would have a super nasty attitude. I would just take my travel pass and go. This went on until she got transferred out of the unit to Long Beach.

But before she left she had one more trick up her sleeve. She told on her boss do you know right before Christmas 2006 I got a phone call to be in the South Central Office in the morning. I agreed the next morning me and my wife was in the supervisor's office. He told us to have a seat then his boss and the female agent walked in. She had a smirk on her face. The supervisor's boss said you will have a Los Angeles County address by next week. We got hit with a hard blow right before Christmas. It was the 20th and I had to move. What could I do and what would I do? I and my wife had to think the female agent smiled and said I have a place for you in Los Angeles. I spoke to her supervisor and asked could I find my own. He said yeah, you have until noon tomorrow. I and my wife began to think. She came up with an excellent idea. She said why don't you get a kitchenette hotel room till you finish your parole the idea was great but where. So it came to me Pomona is L.A. County.

I and my wife jumped in our S.V.V and headed for Pomona. I stopped at the very first one we came to. But for some reason I didn't like it. They wanted almost 400 dollars a week and that was too much. So we went to the next one. I liked it better and it was 100 dollar cheaper. We got it then I had to run to L.A. and show them I had two Los Angeles County address. The female agent was truly shocked. Then I found out that she was being transferred to another unit. They were getting rid of her and her attitude. They had gotten a lot of bad reports concerning her. So she was being moved. I was so happy but I knew that would mean another change for me. Oh well, I was only looking to reach March 11, 2007 now that was my biggest goal.

Then I submitted some paperwork on her because she was still trying to violate me and send me back to prison. She was a cold piece of work, believe me, but I went to her division headquarters and filed a real nice 602 on her. She never should have made those type of threats about, I'll have you locked up. Now I have come to find out that I do have rights. Just because I am a parolee does not take away my rights as a human being.

Now I have been on parole since March 11, 2004 today is January 24, 2007. I have only a very short time left on parole but I was inspired by my lovely wife to write this book about being on parole. No one has ever written a book talking about life on parole. They have books on prison and movies on prison. But what about life, after you collect 200 dollars and have to report to someone who does not even knows you! But has full control over you. No one ever talks about that when you have been to prison and you are honestly trying to put your life back in order. Who is there to honestly help you? The system truly is not set up to help you to get out and do good. Its set to keep you locked up. I hope you have enjoyed this book. I have shared my real life experiences with you. This is not made up of things this really does happen. If you do not believe me just go to prison. I pray you make it through then you can see just what it means to be a parolee.

THE END

www.ingramcontent.com/pod-product-compliance
Lightning Source LLC
Chambersburg PA
CBHW050348290526
45785CB00006B/2684